tourism TATTLER

Issue 11 (NOVEMBER) 2015

PUBLISHER
Tourism Tattler (Pty) Ltd.
PO Box 891, Umhlanga Rocks, 4320
KwaZulu-Natal, South Africa.
Website: www.tourismtattler.com

EXECUTIVE EDITOR Des Langkilde
Cell: +27 (0)82 374 7260
Fax: +27 (0)86 651 8080
E-mail: editor@tourismtattler.com
Skype: tourismtattler

MAGAZINE ADVERTISING

ADVERTISING DIRECTOR Bev Langkilde
Cell: +27 (0)71 224 9971
Fax: +27 (0)86 656 3860
E-mail: bev@tourismtattler.com
Skype: bevtourismtattler

SUBSCRIPTIONS
http://eepurl.com/bocldD

BACK ISSUES (Click on the covers below).

Contents

I0469850

06 EDITORIAL: SA's Visa Regulations Reviewed
10 ACCOLADES: SA's 'Best of the Best'
21 BUSINESS: Responsible Travel in Africa
30 TRANSPORT: Ford Everest Review

IN THIS ISSUE

TRADE NEWS

Visit our website for daily news updates at www.tourismtattler.com

EDITORIAL CONTRIBUTORS

Adv. Louis Nel
Andre du Toit
Des Langkilde
Jennifer Nagy
Kerri Wolter
Prof. Melville Saayman
Sharon van Wyk
Steve Conradie
Unathi Henama

MAGAZINE SPONSORS

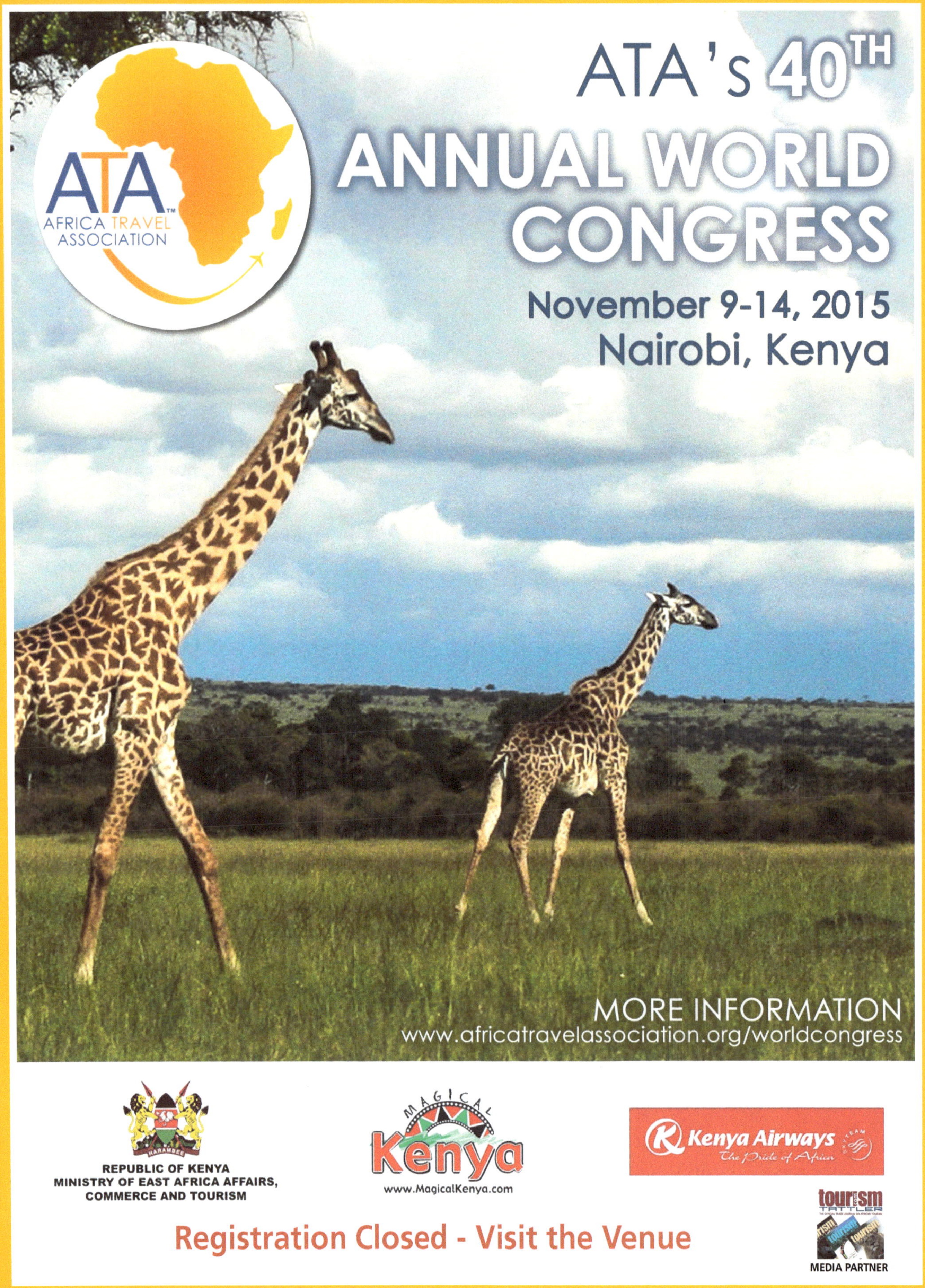

ATA's 40TH
ANNUAL WORLD CONGRESS

November 9-14, 2015
Nairobi, Kenya

MORE INFORMATION
www.africatravelassociation.org/worldcongress

REPUBLIC OF KENYA
MINISTRY OF EAST AFRICA AFFAIRS,
COMMERCE AND TOURISM

www.MagicalKenya.com

MEDIA PARTNER

Registration Closed - Visit the Venue

AFRICAN TRAVEL & TOURISM ASSOCIATION

PROMOTING TOURISM TO
AFRICA
FROM ALL CORNERS OF THE WORLD

Recognised as the Voice of African Tourism, Atta reaches across 22 countries in Africa, showcasing over 530 elite buyers and suppliers of African tourism product.

- Leading role at trade shows around the world
- Networking opportunities
- Industry representation on international commitees & the media
- Interactive platform for information & education
- Daily news service on all aspects of African tourism
- Network of specialist consultants

Join our knowledgeable and experienced membership to increase awareness and visibility of your company

**f attatourism | www.atta.travel | info@atta.travel �

 @atta_tourism**

Lead Sponsor | Working in partnership with Atta

SOUTH AFRICAN AIRWAYS

A STAR ALLIANCE MEMBER ✶

Accreditation

Official Travel Trade Journal and Media Partner to:

The Africa Travel Association (ATA)

Tel: +1 212 447 1357 • Email: info@africatravelassociation.org • Website: www.africatravelassociation.org

ATA is a registered non-profit trade association in the USA, with headquarters in New York and chapters around the world. ATA is dedicated to promoting travel and tourism to Africa and strengthening intra-Africa partnerships. Established in 1975, ATA provides services to both the public and private sectors of the industry. ATA's annual events in the USA and Africa bring industry professionals together to shape Africa's tourism agenda.

The African Travel & Tourism Association (Atta)

Tel: +44 20 7937 4408 • Email: info@atta.travel • Website: www.atta.travel

Members in 22 African countries and 37 worldwide use Atta to: Network and collaborate with peers in African tourism; Grow their online presence with a branded profile; Ask and answer specialist questions and give advice; and Attend key industry events.

National Accommodation Association of South Africa (NAA-SA)

Tel: +2786 186 2272 • Fax: +2786 225 9858 • Website: www.naa-sa.co.za

The NAA-SA is a network of mainly smaller accommodation providers around South Africa – from B&Bs in country towns offering comfortable personal service to luxurious boutique city lodges with those extra special touches – you're sure to find a suitable place, and at the same time feel confident that your stay at an NAA-SA member's establishment will meet your requirements.

Regional Tourism Organisation of Southern Africa (RETOSA)

Tel: +2711 315 2420/1 • Fax: +2711 315 2422 • Website: www.retosa.co.za

RETOSA is a Southern African Development Community (SADC) institution responsible for tourism growth and development. RETOSA's aims are to increase tourist arrivals to the region through. RETOSA Member States are Angola, Botswana, DR Congo, Lesotho, Madagascar, Malawi, Mauritius, Mozambique, Namibia, Seychelles, South Africa, Swaziland, Tanzania, Zambia and Zimbabwe.

Southern Africa Tourism Services Association (SATSA)

Tel: +2786 127 2872 • Fax: +2711 886 755 • Website: www.satsa.com

SATSA is a credibility accreditation body representing the private sector of the inbound tourism industry. SATSA members are Bonded thus providing a financial guarantee against advance deposits held in the event of the involuntary liquidation. SATSA represents: Transport providers, Tour Operators, DMC's, Accommodation Suppliers, Tour Brokers, Adventure Tourism Providers, Business Tourism Providers and Allied Tourism Services providers.

Southern African Vehicle Rental and Leasing Association (SAVRALA)

Contact: manager@savrala.co.za • Website: w

Founded in the 1970's, SAVRALA is the representative voice of Southern Africa's vehicle rental, leasing and fleet management sector. Our members have a combined national footprint with more than 600 branches countrywide. SAVRALA are instrumental in steering industry standards and continuously strive to protect both their members' interests, and those of the public, and are therefore widely respected within corporate and government sectors.

Seychelles Hospitality & Tourism Association (SHTA)

Tel: +248 432 5560 • Fax: +248 422 5718 • Website: www.shta.sc

The Seychelles Hospitality and Tourism Association was created in 2002 when the Seychelles Hotel Association merged with the Seychelles Hotel and Guesthouse Association. SHTA's primary focus is to unite all Seychelles tourism industry stakeholders under one association in order to be better prepared to defend the interest of the industry and its sustainability as the pillar of the country's economy.

International Coalition of Tourism Partners (ICTP)

Website: www.tourismpartners.org

ICTP is a travel and tourism coalition of global destinations committed to Quality Services and Green Growth.

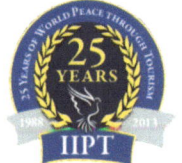

International Institute for Peace through Tourism

Website: www.iipt.org

IIPT is dedicated to fostering tourism initiatives that contribute to international understanding and cooperation.

World Travel Market

WTM Africa - Cape Town in April, WTM Latin America - São Paulo in April, and WTM - London in November. WTM is the place to do business.

World Youth Student and Educational (WYSE) Travel Confederation

Website: www.wysetc.org

WYSE is a global not-for-profit membership organisation.

The Safari Awards

Website: www.safariawards.com

Safari Award finalists are amongst the top 3% in Africa and the winners are unquestionably the best.

World Luxury Hotel Awards

Website: www.luxuryhotelawards.com

World Luxury Hotel Awards is an international company that provides award recognition to the best hotels from all over the world.

Our cover for November pays tribute to the winners of South Africa's 2015 Lilizela Tourism Awards - all of whom are featured in this edition.

The Lilizela Tourism Awards is a platform to celebrate service excellence in the South African tourism industry, and its third annual gala award presentation ceremony, held at the International Convention Centre in Sandton, Johannesburg on 22 October honoured the crème de la crème of the tourism sector.

The Lilizela Tourism Awards have grown substantially since they were launched in 2013. This year, over 1 100 entries were received across all categories – making these awards far reaching and widely representative of the national tourism industry. During the country-wide provincial awards, 219 tourism product owners and service providers in the industry were recognised and rewarded for their contribution to service excellence in tourism and upholding the promise of quality assurance.

South African Tourism Chief Executive Officer, Thulani Nzima congratulated the finalists and winners with a short opening speech: "The contribution of tourism businesses nominated for the Lilizela Tourism Awards keeps the sector on an upward trend. We congratulate all the winners and hope they will continue to serve as tourism ambassadors by continuing to showcase the best of our country to the world as tourism continues to be one of the fastest growing sectors."

Tourism Minister Derek Hanekom demonstrated the country's slogan 'Welcome to our Family' by hugging each award winner as they arrived on stage to receive their trophy and framed certificate. In his speech he congratulated all who work in South Africa's ever growing industry and commended the awardees for contributing in the transformation and growth of the tourism industry.

But the Minister's sentiments on transformation are not shared by everyone. A media statement by Nesang Maleka, Secretary General of 'South African Youth in Travel, Tourism & Hospitality' said "The failure of big business to support and champion these (wholly black owned enterprises) is of great concern. The same attitude big business and organised formations of business in the sector on transformation is clearly mirrored in their absence in the awards." Maleka further refers to the composition of the judging panels ("having [a lack of] young [black] judges"). His sentiments on both counts are wrong, as evidenced by the judging ratio (two thirds black) and the award winners themselves (see featured article on pages 10 - 19).

As a judge myself (in the 1/3 minority ratio) on this years 'Visitor Experience' category, I noticed that quite a few of the smaller entrants lacked basic marketing expertise. For example, their entries lacked social media presence – specifically TripAdvisor, which is essential considering that the judges, having not visited the entrants establishment themselves, have to rely on reviews posted by past clients (amongst other criteria). Perhaps the Lilizela website should note this as a condition of entry when entries open for the 2016 awards in March.

Besides the prestige and media exposure afforded to entrants by winning a Lilizela Tourism Award, I wondered how tourism product buyers view the importance of awards as a decision making factor when selecting or booking ground services, such as accommodation or attractions. For an answer, I asked Thompsons Africa for comment. "When choosing a partner in the tourism industry who has been awarded and recognised for service excellence, you are choosing a partner that will ensure a genuine experience for your guest," replied Viki Haasbroek, Thompsons Marketing Manager.

Whilst this edition celebrates all 2015 Lilizela Tourism Award winners' achievements, our regular content has not been ignored, which includes South Africa's tourism statistics (page 20), a beneficial initiative for Tour Operators who support Fair Trade principles (page 21), an opinion piece on the recent student altercation against colonial remembrance statues (page 22), and three ways to shorten your sales cycle (page 23) in the business section.

The conservation section lambasts Eskom for failing to protect Cape Vultures from colliding with electricity pylons (page 25), while Louis the Lawyer continues his series on contracts (page 26), the professor on all things tourism related expounds on rural regeneration in the marketing section (page 27), and our risk management guru cautions against thunderstorm exposure (page 28).

And finally, our transport section reviews Ford's recently launched Everest SUV (page 30). Of course, this publication would not be able to continue with its policy of free digital distribution without the support of brand display advertising, and in this regard we salute Mercedes-Benz Commercial Vehicles for their ongoing support (page 9). Perhaps Ford South Africa will follow suit in the new future.

Enjoy your reading.

Des Langkilde.

editor@tourismtattler.com

SA's Visa Regulations Reviewed

South Africa's contentious visa and birth certificate regulations have finally been reviewed, but the key question that everyone in the travel trade is asking is 'what now?'

After sixteen months of industry lobbying, South Africa's Deputy President Cyril Ramaphosa, as chairman of the Inter-Ministerial Committee tasked with reviewing South Africa's immigration regulations, has made the right call. In essence he has scrapped the most contentious elements of the visa regulations.

The official cabinet memorandum announcement can be read on the Southern Africa Tourism Services (SATSA) website here.

The key question everyone is asking is 'what now?' Officials from the National Department of Tourism (NDT) are working with Home Affairs to give effect to this cabinet memorandum. Key here is to get absolute clarity on what is required.

"My understanding is that we, in essence, revert to where we were prior to these regulations. There is good news on visa facilitation in China, India, Russia and Nigeria - that accredited agents will play a role in the visa application process and that biometrics will be captured on arrival. The requirement of carrying unabridged birth certificates for inbound travellers falls away. Clarity is definitely required around the term 'strongly advised' (see memorandum links) but my reading is that practical application will revert to the norm when travelling with children, especially when one parent is accompanying them," said SATSA's CEO, David Frost.

According to Trevor Bloem, Chief Director Communications at the NDT, the recommendations will be implemented in a phased approach, and will make it easier for tourists to travel to South Africa without compromising national security or the safety of children.

The following concessions will be implemented in the next three months:

- The Department of Home Affairs will accept visa applications by post in countries where no SA Missions exist.
- Selected travel companies will be accredited to process visa applications on behalf of tourists in China, India and Russia within the next three months. The NDT is assisting the Department of Home Affairs (DHA) to identify suitable companies in these countries to speed up the process. This programme could be extended to other visa requiring countries in the future.

The following will be implemented in the next twelve months:

- Long term multiple entry visas will be issued for business and academic visitors from Africa.
- The DHA will consider a programme which issues visas on arrival for nationals already holding valid visas from the UK, USA, Canada and other countries who undertake stringent checks on visitors.
- Additional Visa Facilitation Centres will be opened in a number of countries to assist with applications for visas and permits.

In the longer term, the DHA will install systems for pre-flight checks at international airports. Advance Passenger Processing systems will be upgraded and a Passenger Name Record will be implemented to enhance risk assessment.

In respect of children from visa-exempt countries, the Cabinet approved a dispensation in terms of which travellers will be strongly advised to bring along proof of the relation and consent from the absent parent/s or guardian/s. This means that Immigration Regulations may require that such documents be produced on arrival in SA. Currently, the status quo remains, until such time that the DHA has facilitated a legal instrument to implement this recommendation.

Travellers from countries where visas are required, provision of original birth certificates or certified copies of required documents should continue during the visa application process. South African children travelling abroad are still required to carry Unabridged Birth Certificates as well as parental consent affidavits from non accompanying parents or guardians.

In addition Cabinet approved the following concessions:

- The validity of the Parental Consent Affidavit will be extended to six months.
- Within the next 3 months school principals will issue letters confirming permission for children to travel on school tours. This authority will also be extended to include registered sports bodies.
- In the next year, the term 'Unabridged Birth Certificate' will be changed to 'Birth Certificate' containing parental details.
- Details of parents will be printed in their children's passports, so that parents would not be required to carry birth certificates.

THE MOST ESTABLISHED, RESPECTED AND RECOGNISED
HOTEL AWARDS BRAND IN THE WORLD

World Luxury Hotel Awards

• GUARANTEED INCREASE IN ANNUAL TURNOVER   • OVER 70 000 WEBSITE HITS PER MONTH
• MARKETING EXPOSURE IN 160 COUNTRIES   • 90 000 TRAVEL SUBSCRIBERS   • SHOWCASE
YOUR HOTEL'S UNIQUE SELLING POINTS   • ATTEND THE EXCLUSIVE ANNUAL BLACK TIE GALA
CEREMONY AND NETWORK WITH THE WORLD'S LEADING HOTELIERS   • WINNERS INCLUDE
900 OF THE WORLD'S LEADING HOTELS, INCLUDING:

BURJ AL ARAB • THE RITZ CARLTON, BERLIN • ATLANTIS THE PALM • CONRAD NEW YORK • HARBOUR GRAND HONG
KONG • SHANGRI-LA HOTEL PARIS • GRAND HOTEL ZERMATTERHOF • INTERCONTINENTAL HANGZHOU
• CONSTANCE HALAVELI MALDIVES

ARE YOU SEARCHING FOR YOUR NEXT LUXURY TRAVEL DESTINATION?
DISCOVER AND BOOK ONE OF OUR INTERNATIONAL
AWARD WINNING HOTELS NOW!

World Luxury
Spa
Awards

WORLD LUXURY HOTEL AWARDS
WWW.LUXURYHOTELAWARDS.COM / +27 21 88 00 345

RECOGNIZING WORLDWIDE
HOSPITALITY EXCELLENCE

World Luxury
Restaurant
Awards

2015 Motor Manufacturer Award

Celebrating its 20th year, the SAVRALA 2015 Manufacturer of the Year (MOTY) was revealed during a gala award ceremony at the Hilton Hotel in Sandton on 23 October. Incredibly, for six consecutive years, Volkswagen South Africa (VW) took the accolade of overall car rental winner yet again.

Commenting on this achievement, SAVRALA President Marc Corcoran applauded VWSA's remarkable achievement and said that one had no choice but to respect the consistent and recognised high levels of service given by VWSA to the car rental industry. "An important insight from this year's data is the improved scores by almost all automotive brands, demonstrating the competitive nature of the industry," he added.

The winners of the SAVRALA awards are decided by the Rental companies such as Avis Budget, Bidvest, Hertz, Europcar / Tempest, First Car, Dollar Thrifty and other rental companies through a scientific and stringent process. SAVRALA members are required to rate 25 motor manufacturers using a survey containing 40 different and targeted questions. The survey covers aspects such as communication, contact with the manufacturer, technical assistance, parts availability and pricing structures.

The MOTY 2015 results further reveal that VWSA has gained a distinct advantage over its peers in Communication and Support.

The competitive nature of this year's MOTY awards was best demonstrated by the 0.1 difference in score between Audi SA and Toyota South Africa Motors which swopped podium places, with Audi taking home silver this year.

Illustrating the extent of how some automotive companies have focused special attention on their car rental customers, the Most Improved Award went to BMW SA which leaped from 11th place last year to 7th this year achieving a phenomenal 17% increase in their 2015 score.

Addressing concerns by some automotive brands that they are at a disadvantage when competing against their larger-volume peers in the car rental industry, a new award called Tutuka was created and won by Audi SA. "The performance of Audi this year clearly demonstrates that winning MOTY is not merely a function of the volumes sold to the car rental industry, but also of satisfying customer needs," said SAVRALA GM Sandile Ntseoane.

The Value Award in its first year was a tight contest, but was won by Ford SA which, by the narrowest of margins, beat VWSA. Commenting further Marc said this ''was an important award as the cost of vehicle ownership is a key consideration for any fleet purchase, whether a corporate fleet or individual purchaser."

MOTY 2015 also acknowledged the role of certain individuals the car rental industry:
- Best Account Executive was won by David Maeko (Ford SA).
- Best Manufacturer's Technical Representative was won by Bennita Senyatsi (Nissan SA).

The MOTY evening also saw industry stakeholders recognise the remarkable service given by Dawn Jones, Imperial Car Rental CEO, who leaves the industry next month after 35 years.

"Dawn leaves behind an incredible legacy that few could even imagine achieving. Ever the shrewd car rental operator, Dawn had a remarkable, innate skill in developing warm relationships with her colleagues, customers and competitors. The industry thanks her for contribution and wishes her well in her future endeavours," concluded Marc.

The VWSA team, from left to right: Carla Wentzel, Nico Fourie, Loshni Pillay, Stanley Netshituka and Petra Hoffmann: Sales and Marketing Director.

A Daimler Brand

SHE SAYS / HE SAYS

"Did you ever think you'd find something that caters to your every need?"

"Yes, the V-Class was worth the wait."

Specifications may vary for the South African market.

JOE PUBLIC IGNITE MBSA/2693/VCL

Welcome to the best of all worlds. Whether you fancy comfort, looks or magnificent handling, the V-Class was made with your needs in mind.

Recognising the 'Best of the Best' in South African Tourism

This year's Lilizela Tourism Awards national gala ceremony recognised 'the Best of the Best' in the South African tourism trade, writes **Des Langkilde**.

Lilizela, an *Nguni* word, meaning to ululate: a uniquely African act of congratulating work well done. Lilizela is a name that truly distinguishes this uniquely South African award.

Having participated again on this years 'Visitor Experience' category judging panel, I'm reminded of the effort and logistics that the organisers put into this prestigious annual industry award.

Aimed at recognising and rewarding the diversity of tourism players and businesses who work passionately and with pride to deliver world-class products and services, and whose delivery grows South Africa's global destination competitiveness, the Lilizela Tourism Awards is an initiative of the National Department of Tourism (NDT), and is delivered by the Tourism Grading Council of South Africa (TGCSA).

The award winners are selected based on the feedback provided by guests, TripAdvisor guest reviews and through the deliberation of a panel of judges for each category.

In my opinion, the organisers and hosts of the Lilizela Tourism Awards - including each provisional tourism authority - can be justifiably proud of their collective efforts in terms of transparency, fairness in the adjudication process and organisation of the award ceremony events, which are akin to the film industry's Oscar Awards, with regional award ceremonies convened in each of South Africa's nine provinces and the final national event held in Johannesburg.

The award process follows four steps, namely; NOMINATING / ENTRY, VOTING, JUDGING and AWARDING.

The travel industry, and more importantly, the consumer of products and services offered by South Africa's tourism industry, are invited to vote for tourism businesses via the website at www.lilizela.co.za. *Note that only tourist guides are nominated, everyone else enters.*

Entries are made under 4 Focus Areas reflecting 8 Categories with the 9th Category being the Minister's Award.

1. Accommodation

The Lilizela Accommodation Awards are designed to encourage and motivate the trade to offer the best service, facilities and product. Entrants have to be a Tourism Grading Council of South Africa graded establishment in order to enter. The categories in this focus area are: Backpacking & Hosteling; Bed & Breakfast; Caravan & Camping; Country House; Game Lodge; Guest House; Hotel; Lodge; Meetings, Exhibitions and Special Events (MESE); Self-catering Exclusive; and Self-catering Shared Vacation.

2. Service Excellence

The Service Excellence - Visitor Experience Awards recognise tourism businesses that enable visitors to experience the diversity that is offered in South Africa. The are 8 categories within the Visitor Experience awards: Roots & Culture; Action & Adventure; Wildlife Encounters; Culture & Lifestyle; Marine Adventure; Scenic Beauty; Beach Experience; and Lap of Luxury.

From 2015 onwards, a Tour Operators Awards category has been introduced to recognise and reward Tour Operators who not only allow tourists to experience the vast authentic experiences in South Africa, but also ensure that the right safety measurements are taken when transporting tourists.

The Tourist Guides Awards category recognises Registered Guides that have gone beyond the call of duty to make a tourist's experience worthwhile, and includes Nature Guides, Adventure Guides and Culture Guides. Unlike the other Service Excellence Awards, the Tourist Guides Awards are nomination based. Visitors or members of the tourism industry are encouraged to nominate tourist guides that have made their experience in South Africa worthwhile.

3. Entrepreneurship

The ETEYA Lilizela Award (Emerging Tourism Entrepreneur of the Year Award) recognises SMME's who have achieved notable success since starting up.

4. Sustainable Development

This focus area includes three categories – Imvelo, Universal Accessibility, and BBB-EE. The Imvelo Awards include: Best Social Involvement Programme, Best Practice Economic Impact, Best Overall Environment Management System and Best Single-Resource Programme (Water, Energy and Waste).

The Minister's Award

This esteemed award recognises outstanding, unique, impactful people, events, and organisations that have performed in a manner that urges the industry closer to tourism's 2020 vision (to grow arrivals to 15 million and create 225 000 new jobs by 2020 with a total direct and indirect GDP contribution target from R189, 4 billion (2009) to R499 billion (2020).

Recognition

The Lilizela Tourism Awards give national recognition to establishments and raise their profile both at home in South Africa and around the world, too. They will bring great publicity and profiling on a number of platforms, including the Tourism Tattler as the following pages attest to.

For more information visit www.lilizela.co.za

MINISTER'S AWARD

Tourism Minister Derek Hanekom announcing Lindiwe Sangweni-Siddo as the recipient of the 2015 Minister's Award. Lindiwe is currently the Managing Director at Birchwood Hotel and OR Tambo Conference Centre, and previously the General Manager at Soweto Hotel on Freedom Square, and Intercontinental Johannesburg Sandton Towers.

ROOTS& CULTURE AWARD

Winner of the Roots & Culture Award, Esther Mahlangu leaving the stage after receiving her trophy from a jubilant Minister Hanekom.

ALL 2015 WINNERS

THE 3RD
LILIZELA
TOURISM AWARDS

IMVELO AWARDS

BEST SOCIAL INVOLVEMENT PROGRAMME

Large Establishments

Aquila Private Game Reserve	Western Cape	Winner	Ⓝ
Abang Africa Travel	Western Cape	1st Runner-up	
Park Inn by Radisson Cape Town Newlands	Western Cape	2nd Runner-up	

Small Establishments

Maliba Lodge	KwaZulu-Natal	Winner	Ⓝ
African Game Lodge	Western Cape	1st Runner-up	

BEST PRACTICE – ECONOMIC IMPACT

Large Establishments

Storms River Adventures	Eastern Cape	Winner	⑰ Ⓝ
Aquila Private Game Reserve	Western Cape	1st Runner-up	
Garden Court Ulundi	KwaZulu-Natal	2nd Runner-up	

Small Establishments

Durban Green Corridor	KwaZulu-Natal	Winner	Ⓝ
Mehloding Community Tourism Trust	Eastern Cape	1st Runner-up	
Maliba Lodge	KwaZulu-Natal	2nd Runner-up	

BEST OVERALL ENVIRONMENTAL MANAGEMENT

Large Establishments

Drakensberg Sun Hotel	KwaZulu-Natal	Winner	Ⓝ
Leriba Hotel & Spa	Gauteng	1st Runner-up	
Sabi River Sun Resort	Mpumalanga	2nd Runner-up	

Small Establishments

Three Trees at Spioenkop	KwaZulu-Natal	Winner	⑰ Ⓝ
Valverde Eco Hotel	Gauteng	1st Runner-up	
T&T Bed and Breakfast	KwaZulu-Natal	2nd Runner-up	

BEST SINGLE RESOURCE MANAGEMENT – WATER

Large Establishments

Teemane / Flamingo Casino	Northern Cape	Winner	Ⓝ
Zebula Golf Estate	Limpopo	1st Runner-up	
Beacon Island Resort	Western Cape	2nd Runner-up	

Small Establishments

Valverde Eco Hotel	Gauteng	Winner	Ⓝ

BEST SINGLE RESOURCE MANAGEMENT – ENERGY

Large Establishments

ATKV - Drakensville Resort	KwaZulu-Natal	Winner	Ⓝ
Aquila Private Game Reserve	Western Cape	1st Runner-up	
Beacon Island Resort	Western Cape	2nd Runner-up	

Small Establishments

Valverde Eco Hotel	Gauteng	Winner	Ⓝ
Three Trees at Spioenkop	KwaZulu-Natal	1st Runner-up	⑰

BEST SINGLE RESOURCE MANAGEMENT – WASTE

Large Establishments

Teemane / Flamingo Casino	Northern Cape	Winner	Ⓝ
Carnival City Casino	Gauteng	1st Runner-up	
Cape Town International Convention Centre	Western Cape	2nd Runner-up	

Small Establishments

Thaba Tshwene Game Lodge	North West	Winner	Ⓝ

INVESTING IN PEOPLE

Large Establishments

The Oyster Box	KwaZulu-Natal	Winner	Ⓝ
The KwaZulu-Natal Sharks Board	KwaZulu-Natal	1st Runner-up	
Park Inn by Radisson Cape Town Newlands	Western Cape	2nd Runner-up	

Note: National Award winners are highlighted. ㉓ See page numbers for more info.

ALL 2015  WINNERS

THE 3RD
LILIZELA
TOURISM AWARDS

ACCOMMODATION AWARDS

KwaZulu-Natal

Happy Hippo Lodge & Backpackers	Backpacking & Hosteling 3-Star	N
Lala Khona Lodge	Bed & Breakfast	
St Lucia Wetlands Guest House	Bed & Breakfast	
Westville B&B	Bed & Breakfast	
Days at Sea Beach Lodge	Country House	
Lythwood Lodge	Country House	
ZuluWaters Shaka Lodge	Game Lodge	
Lodge Afrique	Guest House	
Ammazulu African Palace	Guest House	
Road Lodge Richards Bay	Hotel	
Stayeasy Pietermaritzburg	Hotel 2-Star	N
Garden Court Umhlanga	Hotel	
Southern Sun Elangeni & Maharani	Hotel	
The Oyster Box Hotel	Hotel 5-Star	N
Rain Farm Game and Lodge	Lodge 3-Star	N
Three Trees at Spioenkop	Lodge	
Amakhosi Safari Lodge	Lodge	
Villa La Palma	Self-catering Exclusive	
Cabana Beach Resort	Self-catering Exclusive	

Eastern Cape

Amakhala Quatermain's Camp	Game Lodge	
Apple@Jbay	Self-catering Exclusive	
Duiwekloof Lodge	Self-catering Exclusive	
Dune Ridge Country House	Country House	N
East London International Convention Centre	MESE	
Forest Hall Guest House	Guest House	
Hill Street Manor	Bed & Breakfast	
Longlee Manor	Game Lodge	
Lungile Backpackers	Backpacking & Hosteling	
MyPond Hotel	Hotel	
Pumba Msenge Bush Lodge	Lodge	
River Road Guest House	Bed & Breakfast	
Road Lodge East London	Hotel	
Sibuya Game Reserve - River Camp	Game Lodge 4-Star	N
Tenahead Mountain Lodge & Reserve	Country House	16
The Sands @ St Francis	Guest House	
Tranquil House Bed & Breakfast	Guest House	
Town Lodge Port Elizabeth	Hotel	
Tsitsikamma Lodge & Spa	Hotel	
The Boardwalk Hotel, Convention Centre & Spa	Hotel	
The Fernery Lodge & Chalets	Lodge	
The Oyster Box Beach House	Self-catering Exclusive	
Cape St Francis Resort - Club Break	Self-catering Shared Vacation	
Cape St Francis Beach Break	Self-catering Shared Vacation	N

Western Cape

Atlantic Point Backpackers	Backpacking & Hosteling 4-Star	N
Ocean View B&B	Bed & Breakfast 3-Star	N
Villa Tarentaal	Bed & Breakfast 4-Star	N
Slanghoek Mountain Resort	Caravan & Camping	
Dibiki Holiday Resort	Caravan & Camping 4-Star	N
Grand Dedale Country House	Country House 5-Star	N
De Doornkraal Historic Country House	Country House 4-Star	N
Sanbona Wildlife Reserve - Dwyka Lodge	Game Lodge	
Inyathi Guest Lodge	Guest House	
Dongola House	Guest House	
Villa Afrikana Guest Suites	Guest House	
Eendracht Hotel	Hotel	
Feathers Boutique Hotel	Hotel	
Andros Boutique Hotel	Hotel	
Bushmans Kloof Wilderness Reserve	Lodge 5-Star	N
Van Ryn Distillery and Brandy Cellar	MESE	
The River Siding	Self-catering Exclusive	N
Wolverfontein Cottages	Self-catering Exclusive	
Orange Grove Farm	Self-catering Exclusive	
Hollywood Mansion Camps Bay	Self-catering Exclusive	
ATKV Goudini Spa - Slanghoek Villas	Self-catering Shared Vacation	

Northern Cape

Browns Manor	Bed & Breakfast	
Augrabies Falls National Park	Caravan & Camping	
Mattanu Private Game Reserve	Game Lodge	
Classic Court	Guest House	
African Vineyard Guesthouse	Guest House	
Oleander Guest House	Guest House 5-Star	16 N
Naba Lodge Conference Facility	MESE	
International Convention Solutions	MESE	
Koekais Guest Farm	Self-catering Exclusive	

Free State

Anta Boga Hotel	Hotel	
Art Lovers Guesthouse	Guest House	
Castello Guest House Bloemfontein	Guest House	
De Stijl Gariep Hotel	Hotel 4-Star	14 N
Gariep A Forever Resort Caravan Park	Caravan & Camping	15
Kloof Lodge	Guest House	
Kamohelong Luxury Accommodation	Guest House	
Liedjiesbos B&B	Bed & Breakfast	
Peermont Metcourt Frontier Inn and Casino	Hotel	
Lionsrock Lodge	Lodge	
Letsatsi Game Lodge	Lodge 4-Star	N
Gariep Conferencing A Forever Resort	MESE	15
Mont d'Or Hotel Clarens	MESE	
Mont d'Or Hotel	Hotel	

Gauteng

Askari Lodge and Spa	Guest House	
Terrylin Backpackers	Backpacking & Hosteling 2-Star	N
Hyde Park Villas	Bed & Breakfast 5-Star	N
Oxbow Country Estate	Country House	N
Flamingo's Nest Guest House & Conference Centre	Guest House	
Opikopi Guest House	Guest House	
Liz at Lancaster Guesthouse	Guest House 4-Star	N
Road Lodge Southgate	Hotel	
Town Lodge Roodepoort	Hotel	
Valverde Country Hotel	Hotel	
The Maslow Hotel	Hotel	
RPM Ditsong Conference Center	MESE	
CSIR International Convention Centre	MESE	N
The Forum | The Campus	MESE	
Premiere Classe Suite Hotel	Self-catering Exclusive	
Blue Roan Country Lodge	Self-catering Exclusive	

North West

ATKV Buffelspoort Holiday Resort	Caravan & Camping	
Ivory Tree Game Lodge	Game Lodge	
Franka Guesthouse	Guest House	
Villa Maria Guest Lodge	Guest House	
El Shadai Guesthouse	Guest House	
Road Lodge Potchefstroom	Hotel 1-Star	N
The Royal Marang Hotel	Hotel	
Kassaboera Lodge	Lodge	18
Rio Hotel Casino Convention Resort	MESE 3-Star	
Anne's Place	Self-catering Exclusive	

Mpumalanga

Kgarebana Boutique Bed and Breakfast	Bed & Breakfast 2-Star	N
La Picasso Guesthouse	Bed & Breakfast	
Micasa Luxury Suites	Bed & Breakfast	
Blyde Canyon A Forever Resort Caravan Park	Caravan & Camping 3-Star	15 N
Welgelegen Manor	Country House	
Umlani Bushcamp	Game Lodge 3-Star	21 N
Tintswalo Safari Lodge	Game Lodge 5-Star	19 N
Selati 103 Guest Cottages	Guest House	
Yalla Yalla Boutique Hotel	Guest House	
Ecolux Boutique Hotel	Guest House	
Stayeasy Emnotweni	Hotel	
Pine Lake Inn	Hotel 3-Star	N
Southern Sun Emnotweni	Hotel	

* MESE = Meetings, Exhibitions and Special Events.

Note: National Award winners are highlighted. 23 *See page numbers for more info.*

ALL 2015  WINNERS

THE 3RD
LILIZELA
TOURISM AWARDS

ACCOMMODATION AWARDS

Needles Lodge	Lodge	**Swadini** A Forever Resort Caravan Park	Caravan & Camping ⑮
Summerfields Rose Retreat & Spa	Lodge	Sherwood's Country House	Country House
Ingwenyama Conference & Sports Resort	MESE	Patong Guestlodge	Country House 3-Star Ⓝ
115@Casambo	MESE Ⓝ	Palala Boutique Game Lodge and Spa	Game Lodge
Thaba Tsweni Lodge	Self-catering Exclusive	Vuwa Lodge	Guest House 3-Star Ⓝ
Casambo Self Catering	Self-catering Exclusive	Magoebaskloof Hotel	Hotel
Valbonne House at Tomjachu Bush Lodges	Self-catering Exclusive	Fusion Boutique Hotel	Hotel
Badplaas A Forever Resort Chalets	Self-catering Shared Vacation ⑮	Shangri-La Country Hotel	Hotel
Limpopo		Blyde River Canyon Lodge	Lodge
		Kruger National Park Boulders Private Camp	Self-catering Exclusive
Lapologa Bed and Breakfast	Bed & Breakfast	ATKV Eiland Spa	Self-catering Exclusive

VISITOR EXPERIENCE AWARDS

Island Vibe	(Eastern Cape)	Beach Experience Ⓝ	Shangri-La Country Hotel	(Limpopo)	Scenic Beauty
Mosaic Tourism	(Eastern Cape)	Roots & Culture ⑱	Tshukudu Game Lodge	(Limpopo)	Wildlife Encounters
Khaya Volunteer Projects	(Eastern Cape)	Culture & Lifestyle	Esther Mahlangu Exhibition	(Mpumalanga)	Roots & Culture Ⓝ
Tsitsikamma Segway Tours	(Eastern Cape)	Scenic Beauty Ⓝ	Gods Window	(Mpumalanga)	Scenic Beauty Ⓝ
Koffylaagte Game Lodge	(Eastern Cape)	Wildlife Encounters	Inyati Game Lodge	(Mpumalanga)	Wildlife Encounters Ⓝ
SRA - Tsitsikamma Canopy Tours	(Eastern Cape)	Action & Adventure Ⓝ	**Induna Adventures**	(Mpumalanga)	Action & Adventure ⑱
Untouched Adventures	(Eastern Cape)	Marine Adventure ⑥	The Ann Van Dyk Cheetah Centre - DeWildt	(North West)	Wildlife Encounters
Cheetah Experience	(Free State)	Wildlife Encounters	Harties Cableway	(North West)	Action & Adventure
Maropeng A' Afrika Leisure	(Gauteng)	Roots & Culture ⑰	The Big Hole Kimberley	(Northern Cape)	Roots & Culture
Tso's Butchery and Fast Food	(Gauteng)	Culture & Lifestyle Ⓝ	Richards Supper Stage and Bistro	(Western Cape)	Roots & Culture
Soulstice Day Spa	(Gauteng)	Lap of Luxury	Gold Restaurant	(Western Cape)	Culture & Lifestyle Ⓝ
Johannesburg Skydiving Club	(Gauteng)	Action & Adventure	Table Mountain Aerial Cableway	(Western Cape)	Scenic Beauty
Amakhosi Safari Lodge	(KwaZulu-Natal)	Wildlife Encounters	Tenikwa Wildlife Awareness & Rehabi Cntr	(Western Cape)	Wildlife Encounters
The Oyster Box Hotel	(KwaZulu-Natal)	Lap of Luxury Ⓝ	Marine Dynamics Tours	(Western Cape)	Marine Adventure Ⓝ
Wild 5 Adventures	(KwaZulu-Natal)	Action & Adventure	Gravity Adventures	(Western Cape)	Action & Adventure
Ushaka Marine World	(KwaZulu-Natal)	Marine Adventure			

TOUR OPERATOR AWARDS

African Heartland Journeys	(Eastern Cape)	Established	Access2africa Safaris	(KwaZulu-Natal)	Emerging Ⓝ
Mosaic Tourism	(Eastern Cape)	Emerging ⑱	kay 2ze gee Tours	(North West)	Emerging
Thabile Tours and Shuttle	(Free State)	Emerging	Ilios Travel	(Western Cape)	Emerging
Ulysses Tours & Safaris	(Gauteng)	Established Ⓝ	Propel Africa Destination Management	(Western Cape)	Established
Buja Tours	(Gauteng)	Emerging			

TOURIST GUIDE AWARDS

Craig Ronald Duffield	(Eastern Cape)	Culture Guides ⑱	Raymond Khosa	(Mpumalanga)	Nature Guide
Martie Craig	(Free State)	Culture Guides	Samuel Seleke	(North West)	Nature Guide
Carmen Michelle Sonnenberg	(Gauteng)	Culture Guides	Annelize Magrietha Grimbeek	(North West)	Adventure Guide
Duval Pierre	(KwaZulu-Natal)	Nature Guides	Romano Sylvester Bezuidenhout	(Northern Cape)	Culture Guide
Jeffrey Mthandeni Buthelezi	(KwaZulu-Natal)	Culture Guide	Steven Bolnik	(Western Cape)	Nature Guide
Michael Keith Henry Jones	(Limpopo)	Nature Guide Ⓝ	Charles Howell	(Western Cape)	Culture Guide
Nelson Maphaha	(Limpopo)	Culture Guide Ⓝ			

UNIVERSAL ACCESSIBILITY AWARDS

Access2Africa Safaris	KwaZulu-Natal	Accomm Mobility Ⓝ	Hluleka Nature Reserve	Eastern Cape	Accomm Mobility
Access2Africa Safaris	KwaZulu-Natal	Accomm Hearing Ⓝ	Holiday Inn Johannesburg	Gauteng	General UA Ⓝ
Access2Africa Safaris	KwaZulu-Natal	Accomm Mobility Ⓝ	**Soli deo Gloria**	Western Cape	Accomm Mobility ⑱ Ⓝ
Garden Court Ulundi	KwaZulu-Natal	Accomm Mobility	The Big Hole	Northern Cape	Accomm Mobility

ETEYA AWARDS

Simeliza Tours	Mpumalanga	Winner Ⓝ	MTS Travel t/a My Travel	KwaZulu-Natal	
Chavonnes Battery	Western Cape	1st Runner Up	Lerato Travel Agency	North West	
GreenSA Travel Centre	Limpopo	2nd Runner Up	Fusion Garden Restaurant	Gauteng	
Xhobani MultiPurpose Primary Cooperative	Eastern Cape	3rd Runner Up			

B-BBEE AWARDS

Khol Newman Bed and Breakfast	Eastern Cape	Exempted Micro Enterprise (EME) 0 – R2.5 Mil	Ⓝ
SRA - Tsitsikamma Canopy Tours	Eastern Cape	Qualifying Small Enterprise (QSE) R2.5 – R3.5 Mil	Ⓝ
Sun International Group	Gauteng	Large Enterprise R35 Mil <	Ⓝ

* MESE = Meetings, Exhibitions and Special Events.
Note: National Award winners are highlighted. ㉓ **See page numbers for more info.**

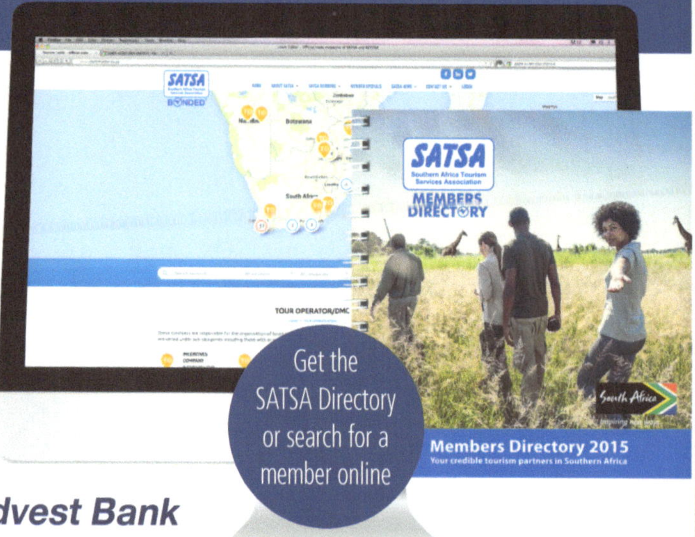

Voted
SOUTH AFRICA'S BEST

THE 3RD
LILIZELA
TOURISM AWARDS

"Where else in the World..."

TINTSWALO

SAFARI LODGE

Settled on the unfenced western boundary of South Africa's renowned Kruger National Park, at what seems the very heart of the African bush, lies the private Manyeleti Game Reserve. Sharing this vast wilderness with only two other commercial lodges, the luxurious five-star Tintswalo Safari Lodge is perfectly located to offer all the raw, natural beauty of Africa, without the usual tourist crowds.

Whether in search of a safari expedition, or sublime wilderness retreat, Tintswalo Safari Lodge transports guests to a place where indulgence is the norm and expectations are met with effortless discretion and grace.

+27 (0)11 300 8888 | res2@tintswalo.com
Manyeleti Game Reserve, Greater Kruger
www.tintswalo.com

HONOURING
THE BEST
OF THE BEST

South Africa

THE
LILIZELA
TOURISM AWARDS
2015

Tintswalo Safari Lodge was announced National Winner of the 2015 Lilizela Award in the Five-Star Game Lodge category!

Market Intelligence Report

The information below was extracted from data available as at **02 November 2015**. By **Martin Jansen van Vuuren** of **Grant Thornton**.

ARRIVALS

The latest available data from **Statistics South Africa** is for **January to July 2015***:

	Current period	Change over same period last year
UK	227 323	0.5%
Germany	128 346	-9.3%
USA	166 759	-6.7%
India	45 973	-13.5%
China (incl Hong Kong)	40 953	-29.1%
Overseas Arrivals	1 149 253	-8.7%
African Arrivals	3 88 625	-5.8%
Total Foreign Arrivals	5 040 116	-6.4%

HOTEL STATS

The latest available data from **STR Global** is for **January** to **September 2015**:

Current period	Average Room Occupancy (ARO)	Average Room Rate (ARR)	Revenue Per Available Room (RevPAR)
All Hotels in SA	61.9%	R 1 057	R 654
All 5-star hotels in SA	61.3%	R 1 901	R 1 166
All 4-star hotels in SA	60.9%	R 1 000	R 609
All 3-star hotels in SA	62.0%	R 861	R 533
Change over same period last year			
All Hotels in SA	0.9%	5.9%	6.9%
All 5-star hotels in SA	0.3%	8.2%	8.5%
All 4-star hotels in SA	1.8%	5.2%	7.1%
All 3-star hotels in SA	-0.8%	6.2%	5.3%

ACSA DATA

The latest available data from **ACSA** is for **January** to **September 2015**:

Change over same period last year	Passengers arriving on International Flights	Passengers arriving on Regional Flights	Passengers arriving on Domestic Flights
OR Tambo International	-0.7%	-2.8%	9.1%
Cape Town International	8.7%	8.2%	7.8%
King Shaka International	-5.3%	N/A	4.9%

CAR RENTAL DATA

The latest available data from **SAVRALA** is for **January to June 2015**:

	Current period	Change over same period last year
Industry rental days	8 139 127	-1%
Industry utilisation	70.2%	-0.7%
Industry Average daily revenue	2 498 944 728	1%

WHAT THIS MEANS FOR MY BUSINESS

The Statistics South Africa data shows the negative impact of the visa regulations on international arrivals to South Africa. Hotel occupancies have been maintained, while rates increase off the back of the domestic tourism market as reflected in the growth in passengers arriving on domestic flights. *Note that African Arrivals plus Overseas Arrivals do not add to Total Foreign Arrivals due to the exclusion of unspecified arrivals, which could not be allocated to either African or Overseas. As from January 2014, Stats SA has stopped counting people transiting through SA as tourists. As a result of the revision, in order to compare the 2014 figures with 2013, it is necessary to deduct the transit figures from the 2013 totals.*

For more information contact Martin at Grant Thornton on +27 (0)21 417 8838 or visit: http://www.gt.co.za

How to Support Responsible Travel in Africa

Tour operators play a major role in influencing responsible travel through the holiday packages they design and offer to clients. Your business can support responsible travel in Africa by promoting Fair Trade Tourism certified tourism products and by packaging and selling Fair Trade Holidays, writes **Sharon van Wyk**.

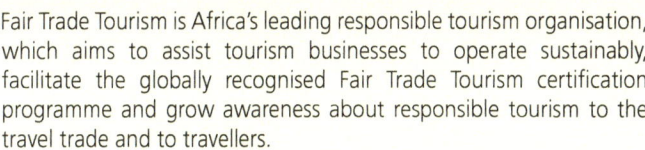

Fair Trade Tourism is Africa's leading responsible tourism organisation, which aims to assist tourism businesses to operate sustainably, facilitate the globally recognised Fair Trade Tourism certification programme and grow awareness about responsible tourism to the travel trade and to travellers.

Fair Trade Tourism certified tourism businesses use the Fair Trade Tourism label to signify their commitment to fair wages and working conditions, fair purchasing and operations, equitable distribution of benefits and respect for human rights, culture and the environment.

The certification standard, encompassing 200 criteria, represents the global benchmark in responsible tourism and is the first standard in Africa to be recognised by the Global Sustainable Tourism Council.

Fair Trade Tourism currently has certification programmes in South Africa, Madagascar and Mozambique, together with mutual recognition agreements with Tanzania and Seychelles, and is currently assessing an agreement with Namibia. Mutual recognition is a process through which the standards of two certification schemes are assessed as equivalent.

Fair Trade Tourism is currently expanding its scope and influence in Africa as well as in key international source markets in Europe and the USA. Aims and efforts are focused on:

- Increasing the number of Fair Trade Tourism certified products in Southern Africa;
- Increasing the supply of certified sustainable tourism products in Africa through mutual recognition agreements with similar certification schemes.
- Promoting Fair Trade Holidays to package and sell sustainable tourism products in the international market-place.
- Expanding the numbers of tour operators approved by Fair Trade Tourism to sell Fair Trade Holidays.

Tour Operator Approval Process

To be approved by Fair Trade Tourism, Tour operators need to pledge their support to Fair Trade Tourism's principles and agree to package and promote holidays in which at least 50% of the bed-nights featured are spent in tourism establishments that are certified by Fair Trade Tourism or by a mutually recognised certification scheme in Africa.

There are three ways in which a tour operator can be approved:

- If you are already a Tourcert certified operator, you will be automatically approved to package and sell Fair Trade Holidays as a result of a formal mutual recognition agreement signed between Fair Trade Tourism and TourCert in 2013.
- If you are already a Travelife certified operator, you will also be automatically approved to package and sell Fair Trade Holidays.
- If you wish to be independently approved, you need to sign the Fair Trade Tourism Code of Conduct, which commits your business to fair, transparent and sustainable business practices, fair supplier relationships, transparency with customers, and active support of Fair Trade Tourism Holidays and products.
- You will also need to display your commitment to the Fair Trade Tourism Code of Conduct on your website and marketing collateral and you will need to demonstrate this commitment by providing supporting documentation if required.

There are considerable benefits to becoming a Fair Trade Tourism approved tour operator, including:

- Playing a lead role in promoting sustainable tourism suppliers to discerning travellers;
- Enhancing your credibility by displaying the Fair Trade Tourism Approved and Fair Trade Holiday logos in your promotional material and website;
- Increasing market access by being showcased on the Fair Trade Tourism website and other Fair Trade Tourism marketing channels;
- Working with fellow operators to promote Fair Trade Tourism through the value chain.

If you are already a Tourcert or Travelife certified operator, notify us and we will send you a label use agreement to sign which entitles you to use the Fair Trade Tourism Approved and Fair Trade Holiday logos.

For independent approval, contact us for a copy of the Fair Trade Tourism Code of Conduct, sign it and return it. For more information on Fair Trade Tourism visit *www.fairtrade.travel*

For more information contact the programme development manager, Manuel Bollmann, at *manuel@fairtrade.travel* or call 012 342 2945.

Paul Kruger Must Fall, Paul Kruger Must Rise

The acts of statue vandalism that have beset South Africa this year highlight the need for the country to protect its cultural heritage for tourism growth, writes **Unathi Sonwabile Henama**.

The statue of Afrikaner hero Paul Kruger, located at the centre of Church Square in Pretoria, was defaced for a second time with green paint. This act of vandalism occured just after October 10th, which celebrates Kruger Day, and mere months after the statue of Cecil John Rhodes was smeared with human excrement and removed from the University of Cape Town on April 9th.

These acts of vandalism have occured in a year that South Africans are increasingly debating their collective heritage. The ANC Youth League (ANCYL) in Tshwane, led by Lesego Makhubela has called for the removal of the statue of Paul Kruger from Church Square, while the Rekord newspaper reports that the David Motsamai branch of the ANCYL has also called for the removal of the statue and are apparently preparing to organise a march to agitate for its removal and replace it with statues of the Rivonia Trialists. The trial was named after Rivonia, the suburb of Johannesburg where 19 ANC leaders had been arrested at Liliesleaf Farm, privately owned by Arthur Goldreich, on 11 July 1963. Today, Lilliesleaf is a major tourist attraction and a site of national significance. The Rivonia trialists were charged and convicted to life imprisonment at Robben Island.

A memorial of Rivonia trialist statues on Church Square, in front of the court that sentenced them to life imprisonment, would increase the number of tourists that visit the city centre and increase on the other hand, police visibility in the CBD to the mutual benefit of locals and tourists alike. The "Mandela magic" always increases tourist arrivals – you need only ask the Mangaung Municipality and the erection of the Statue of Nelson Mandela at Naval Hill, that was donated by Freddy Kenny, to attest to this fact. The increase in tourist arrivals in the city centre would also reduce the negative impacts of gentrification and increase property prices.

There can be no denying the fact that before 1994, there was Afrikaner hegemony in public displays of culture and heritage. In a paper titled Transforming Tourism: Black Empowerment, Heritage and Identity beyond Apartheid, it is noted that "much of South Africa's cultural infrastructure, such as monuments and museums, reflect the needs and interests of the white minority, focusing on aspects of colonial heritage rather than offering a more diverse and sensitive portrayal of South African history. Sabine Marschall in her publication titled 'Making Money with Memories' noted that monuments and memorials "speak" through their symbols, visual signifiers and textual inscriptions. The post apartheid government continues to create statues, monuments and murals to speak about

the struggle for liberation. In a paper, 'The Impact of Politics of Heritage and Cultural Tourism', Jackie Grobler notes that heritage and tourism are closely linked to a country's past and this turbulent past is characterised by intergroup contests for supremacy, military conflict, economic exploitation and cultural expression. This leads to the politicisation of the past, but in this contestation it must be understood that heritage is a product for tourism consumption.

We must not be caught with our eyes off the ball, ours is about using the different heritages to attract money from tourists to address the challenges of poverty, inequality and unemployment.

I will be the first one to call that the statue of Paul Kruger must fall, and be the first to call for the statue of Paul Kruger to rise. South Africa remains a deeply divided nation, therefore Thabo Mbeki's two nation's speech in 1996 still resonates. Far too many times the sociology of public discourse in South Africa been defined by lack of appreciation of divergent views. There are people that regard Paul Kruger as a hero, and they must have space to appreciate their hero in a befitting setting. In an article by Adam Wakefiled, titled 'Voortrekker Monument willing to take Kruger statue', the statue of Pretoria can be moved to the Voortrekker Monument, as long as its not lost as part of the heritage of Tshwane. The city is large enough to provide a platform for using different heritages to lead to greater tourism consumption. Heritage must bring us together instead of dividing us. What is imperative is that this common heritage must increase the financial benefit for the citizens of Tshwane. The City of Tshwane has recently launched the Tshwane National Heritage Monument at Groenkloof with the aim of erecting more than 400 life sized bronze statues of pre-colonial, colonial and anti-apartheid struggle figures. The beauty about the South Africa is that the preamble to the Constitution is clear that "South Africa belongs to all that live in it, united in our diversity". Therefore Paul Kruger must fall, and Paul Kruger must rise. In tourism economics we seek a win-win situation, let them see Paul Kruger and let them see the Rivonia Trialists. Can't we just get along?

About the Author: Unathi Sonwabile Henama *teaches tourism in the Department of Tourism Management at the Tshwane University of Technology. The views expressed in this article are private. Unathi can be contacted via email at: HenamaUS@tut.ac.za or by calling: +27 (0)12 382 5507.*

Three Ways to Shorten Your Sales Cycle

Every company's ultimate goal is financial success (a.k.a. profitability) but many find it difficult to maintain, especially when their product or service has a lengthy sales cycle, writes **Jennifer Nagy**.

Here are three ways that a B2B business can shorten their sales cycle:

1. Educate potential customers

The first step in the customer buying cycle is 'need recognition', in which the potential customer decides that they need to find a solution to address a specific problem that they are experiencing. Although some customers might already know about the solution that exists, most potential customers will have little to no knowledge about the variety of options available to them. Without proper understanding of the need that the offering fulfils and the specific benefits that a property can expect to achieve using the product or service, closing the sale will be next to impossible.

This is your opportunity to educate potential clients about the issue (that your company's solution solves), including why it happens, how it can be prevented, and possible solutions that will eliminate the issue. Keep in mind that this is not the time to sell your product or service specifically; instead, provide a high-level overview of the issue and the available solutions on the market. By being the company who provides educational, unbiased information about ALL of the possible solutions, a potential client is more likely to trust your company – and therefore, is more likely to select you as their service provider.

2. Increase brand awareness

Brand awareness is a key component of a successful sales strategy. Once a customer has determined that they have a need, they will first consider any companies that they know of that provide the necessary product or service (before undertaking research into the other companies offering similar services). Of course, that means that if your company has good brand awareness with decision-makers at hotels, you will receive more warm leads (a.k.a. opportunities to sell).

As well as increasing the number of leads that your company receives, a potential customer's prior knowledge of the company will be advantageous during the final decision-making process. Most potential customers value a company with a strong reputation and a familiar product/service more greatly, than an unknown company.

3. Build credibility in the industry

It is important that potential customers have a favourable impression of your company. By continuing to provide a high-quality product or service to every customer, publicizing your company's good news and executing a strong brand awareness campaign, your B2B company will be able to positively influence the credibility that your company has in the minds' of potential customers.

So, how do you go about implementing the above?

Public relations (PR) and content marketing are the most effective marketing tactics available to educate potential customers, grow brand awareness and build credibility within the industry. Using PR, a company pitches stories and information to journalists about their company, product or service, in an attempt to secure editorial coverage. For example, a B2B company that has created a brand new RMS could contact trade journalists to let them know about the new operational trend that the RMS will create in the industry (because the tech will completely change how hotels execute revenue management going forward).

Content marketing is a marketing tactic in which a company creates and distributes educational, engaging content with the purpose of driving action. This content can be shared via a variety of mediums, such as on the company blog, through social media, in email newsletters sent out to the company's marketing list, reprinted in notable online trade publications, such as Tourism Tattler. With content marketing, the more people who read the content, the greater the credibility and brand awareness that the company will create in the minds' of potential customers.

Ideally, the two tactics should be implemented on an ongoing basis using consistent messaging to ensure a significant increase in the company's credibility with potential customers and increase brand and product awareness, which will result in a shorter sales cycle, more leads and eventually, greater revenue.

Editor's note: To ensure that your PR practitioners content gets published, budget for advertising support. PR company's are good at writing engaging content and rely on media publishers to distribute this to their readers. The two go hand-in-hand – good content supported with strong visual brand awareness equals lead generation.

About the author: Jennifer Nagy *is the President of JLNPR, a full-service public relations and marketing agency that lives and breathes all facets of the travel technology industry. From online travel agencies to revenue management systems, tablet-based aviation automation solutions to IFE technology, hotels to airlines and everything in between, JLNPR uses our knowledge and experience to get your B2B travel technology company noticed by media, influencers and potential customers. For more ingo visit* www.jlnpr.com *or contact Jennifer at* jenn@jlnpr.com

Competition

'Like' / 'Share' / 'Connect' with these Social Media icons to win!

The winning 'Like' or 'Share' during the month of **November 2015** will receive a
Rainbow Nation Navigation Book + a hand crafted Leather Bracelet with red beading with the compliments of
Livingstones Supply Co – *Suppliers of the Finest Products to the Hospitality Industry*.

Livingston Supply Company

Tourism Tattler

Competition Rules: Only one winner will be selected each month on a random selection draw basis. The prize winner will be notified via social media. The prize will be delivered by the sponsor to the winners postal address within South Africa. Should the winner reside outside of South Africa, delivery charges may be applicable. The prize may not be exchanged for cash.

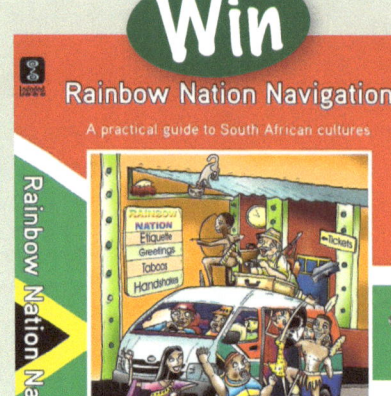

An abundance of cultures and 11 official languages makes interacting with South Africans very complicated. While you're wondering why someone behaves so strangely, they may be thinking the same thing about you! We need practical guidance to help us understand our diverse cultures, and 'Rainbow Nation Navigation' offers exactly that.

Price: R212.28 (R242.00 incl VAT)

Congratulations to our October Social Media winner

Winner

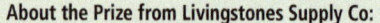

@LodgeShots

Lodge Shots - Specialists in lodge and hotel photography in Africa has been selected as our **October 2015** winner for their 'Follow' on **Twitter.**
Lodge Shots will receive a **Home Classix Solar Lantern** with the compliments of **Livingstones Supply Co –** *Suppliers of the Finest Products to the Hospitality Industry.*

About the Prize from Livingstones Supply Co:
Home Classix is an eco-friendly and stylish Solar Lantern. This solar lantern is supplied with a 18650 lithium battery (900 MAH). The lantern will operate for 5 to 7 hours once fully charged. The 15 LED lights can last up to 100 000 hours.

For more information visit www.livingstonessupplyco.com

Eskom Carnage On Vultures Continues

The recent discovery of another 4 Cape vultures found electrocuted by the Eskom distribution network in the Eastern Cape, should ring alarm bells for the environmental management division of Eskom, writes **Kerri Wolter**.

The South African Electricity Supply Commission (Eskom) network of power lines are known to have a detrimental effect on the Vultures (specifically the Cape vulture) and raptor populations with many of the birds being either maimed or electrocuted. Other species affected by this power line network include species like the cranes, bustards and storks.

Vultures in Africa are decreasing at an alarming rate with multiple threats causing a steep decline in their numbers. One of these being the negative impact the Eskom grid has on the survival of the vultures.

Cape Vultures are classified as regionally endangered and globally vulnerable with under 4000 breeding pairs left. The Cape Vulture is the only endemic vulture species to southern Africa and has already become extinct as a breeding species in Namibia, Zimbabwe and Swaziland.

During 2015 Vulpro has been inundated with maimed birds due to a direct negative interaction with the Eskom network. A large percentage of these birds collide with the infrastructure resulting in permanent wing damage. The majority of these vultures will never be able to be released. In addition to this a large number of electrocuted birds have been reported. Should this trend continue, the Cape Vulture in particular, will face imminent extinction.

Eskom has a history of re-active mitigation as opposed to pro-active mitigation and continues to operate largely in this manner. Despite numerous pleas for this attitude to change, this manner of 'treating' the problem continues to operate. It is now more than ever, vital that Eskom become more active in preventing the total decline of all vulture populations in Southern Africa.

Vulpro will continue to tackle conservation of African vulture populations for the benefit and well-being of society, however expects that Eskom will improve their approach and attitude towards improving the status of their infrastructure to minimise the negative affect it is having on the vulture populations of South Africa.

For more information email kerri.wolter@gmail.com or visit the Vulpro website at www.vulpro.com

Legal

FROM THE BENCH™

With Louis the Lawyer
BENCHMARK ©

RISK IN TOURISM

– PART 15 –

THE LAW: CONTRACTS

REQUISITE #10: ENFORCING YOUR CONTRACT – PART 1

Homework – What To Do Before You Go Ahead

Words loosely used and sometimes with dire financial consequences are: *'I'll see you in court'* and *'(Don't talk to me) talk to my lawyer'*. This is all good and well, but have you done your homework?

This article and the next four inserts will assist and guide you by providing steps to take before you 'shoot your mouth off' and even before you brief your own lawyers, if AT ALL!

'Yes' it is imperative that you yourself know where you stand in the Russian Roulette of litigation – as I've often said: it is very good business and risk management strategy to know and understand your own risk and to address it yourself first and this is especially important with litigation – the minute you brief your attorneys the clock starts ticking and if you look at fees of around R3 000 an hour, that means R50 per minute so do your homework as per my guidelines/checklist and you can save yourself mega bucks e.g. you may find that there is no need to brief your lawyer at all as (1) You may have a very weak case and/or (2) It may be completely feasible to pursue an amicable settlement (either as an alternative to or before litigating)!

This 'homework' comprises 6 steps and we will deal with them in this and subsequent issues: (1) How enforceable is your contract? (2) Have the requisites been met? (3) What are the options available? (4) Preparation (5) Implementation and (6) Mitigating your damages.

1. How Enforceable Is Your Contract?

This question must be addressed from two perspectives namely, commercial and legal.

The commercial question is simply the following: go thru the contract or if available, the executive summary (See previous articles re latter) and prepare a checklist of each party's expectations and deliverables, then work thru it and see whether these have been met. Discussions with managers and site visits may be required but the important aspect is that you need to know whether you can go into the dispute without fearing a 'counter-attack' from the other party based on poor or non-performance. The exercise thus requires a degree of introspection and objectivity – don't go 'shooting from the hip' only to find out that 'your own house is not in order': it can be very costly so rather slow down, do your homework and if there are shortcomings, find out for yourself.

The legal question, over and above issues such as *locus standi*, jurisdiction etc means to have to go back to the basics and that is: have requisites for a binding contract been met?

2. Have The Requisites Been Met?

The first question is has there been a clear and definitive offer and acceptance? As we now know for example a qualified acceptance is not acceptance, it is a counter-offer which in itself must be accepted. This example is often found with lease agreements for premises where the letting agent will provide the potential lessee with an offer to rent/lease document which is often not duly completed or contains a suspensive condition such as '*This offer is subject to the lessor's standard lease agreement being entered into*' – the latter should be vetted before the rental offer is signed.

The second question is whether the 'contract' the parties have entered into constitutes a legally binding obligation. It may well be that the agreement is contra bonos mores i.e. against the norms and morals of society and thus not enforceable. Creditors are often frustrated by the legal system and sometimes a debt is very hard to collect if a debtor simply digs in his/her heels and refuses to pay. As a consequence a creditor may engage the services of a debt collector – if the latter operates within the parameters of the law and provides a legally recognized service, then it will be all good and well and the contract enforceable. However from time to time businesses engage the services of *'rogue debt collectors'* and pay a huge upfront deposit – the latter is based on the outcome but this outcome the debt collector attempts to achieve by illegal means such as blackmail, extortion and sometimes with not so subtle threats of physical violence. If the debt is then not collected, the business will fail in its endeavour to recover the deposit as the contract per se is not enforceable – this is because society does not concede creditors taking the law into their own hands.

How Tourism Can Lead To Rural Area Regeneration

Creative packaging and marketing of rural tourism attractions can lead to job creation and rural regeneration, writes **Prof. Melville Saayman**.

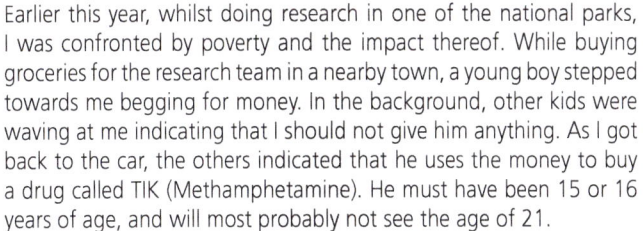

Earlier this year, whilst doing research in one of the national parks, I was confronted by poverty and the impact thereof. While buying groceries for the research team in a nearby town, a young boy stepped towards me begging for money. In the background, other kids were waving at me indicating that I should not give him anything. As I got back to the car, the others indicated that he uses the money to buy a drug called TIK (Methamphetamine). He must have been 15 or 16 years of age, and will most probably not see the age of 21.

This is the case of many kids in rural towns in South Africa, and made me realise that as a tourism industry, especially in rural areas, we need to take responsibility and make a difference. Many rural towns are under growing pressure due to: Urbanisation; Lack of basic services; Bad municipal management Changes in agriculture due to a change from family-owned to commercially-owned farming; Poor land use management; Inadequate planning; Environmental degradation; High levels of unemployment and low income households; High leakages; and Degradation of infrastructure.

However, most small towns in places such as the Karoo and other rural areas in the Northern Cape, KwaZulu-Natal, North West, Limpopo and Eastern Cape have much to offer tourists, such as historical buildings and sites, cultural tourism, ecotourism and agritourism to name a few. Through tourism one could not only create jobs, but careers for people and most importantly create wealth.

Wealth creation leads to job creation, and not the other way around, which is something that few people understand. The reason I stress careers rather than just jobs is that a career requires training and development and it is my belief that the only way to reduce poverty is to empower people.

Which brings me to the opportunities that are available in order to regenerate rural areas.

First of all, like any successful business venture, you need a champion to kick start the regeneration of small towns. Then do an inventory of what is available, and most towns have a few citizens who know exactly what is available and the stories that form part of the heritage products. This will form the bases of the marketing drive, if it has not been done before.

Focus on unique products and attractions and be creative in order to package what is available in an attractive manner. Once again I stress the concept of being creative. I have unfortunately seen so many strategies done at national, provincial and local level by large consulting firms, and have to admit that they showed little to no creativity. This, however, is only one part of the story.

The second part is the part that can create jobs and really make a significant contribution to grow and regenerate the local economy and town in general. It is here that creativity really becomes paramount and requires an integration of what the town and the region have to offer.

Here are just a few examples:

The first possibility is to marry the towns' tourism potential with agritourism. The latter is most probably one of the largest underutilised growth areas in the tourism industry. The Western Cape has followed this strategy with great success, especially if one looks at integrating wine, milk (cheese) and berry farming with tourism. This had huge spinoffs for smaller towns that became touristic towns. The Red Berry Farm outside George and Fairview near Paarl are just two examples of agritourism in action.

In the second possibility, the focus is on arts and culture and how this can transform a rural tourism town into something exciting. One of the best examples is Clarens in the Free State where various artists live and work and has subsequently become a top tourist destination.

A third possibility is to focus on activities, and the one that I am using as an example is fly fishing. Once again we have a wonderful success story with Dullstroom in Mpumalanga, where the availability of trout became the foundation of a tourist destination, with a huge spillover effect in town.

These are just a few possibilities that prove how sleepy towns can be regenerated to become top tourist destinations. Most of these towns also use festivals to ensure that they retain or grow their markets. We have so many existing case studies to work from and much potential in rural areas, maybe it is time that we start to focus stronger on these areas and grow tourism where it is really needed in order to continue to address poverty and create hope for young people that desperately need it. I strongly believe that this is an underdeveloped area in South Africa that can offer domestic and international tourists something new and exciting.

About the Author: Professor Melville Saayman is currently director of the research focus area TREES (Tourism Research in Economic Environs and Society) at the North-West University (Potchefstroom Campus) in South Africa. From his pen, numerous leisure and tourism books (20), scientific articles (110), technical reports (300) and in-service training manuals (8) have been published.
For more information visit www.nwuexperts.co.za

Thunderstorm Season

As summer approaches the Southern Hemisphere it is important to listen for storm warnings. Weather conditions change rapidly and thunderstorms are especially prevalent at this time of the year, writes **Andre du Toit**.

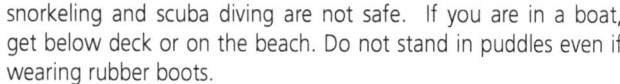

Objects struck by lightning experience heat and magnetic forces of great magnitude and could prove fatal. By way of example, the resultant electric current from a single lightning bolt can provide enough energy to light a city of 200 000 people for one minute!

Below are some guidelines of what to do before, during and after a lightning storm.

When you see lightning or a thunderstorm approaching:

- Get inside a building or an enclosed vehicle. Keep away from windows and open doors. If you are outdoors, go to low ground and crouch down. If you are in a group, stay several yards apart from one another. If there is no shelter, crouch in a low area with low brush or bushes. Lightning often strikes the tallest object. Never crouch beneath tall trees.

- Avoid standing near water, tall objects (including trees or poles) and metal objects. Electrical current can easily travel through them and then to you. Stay out of the water. Never go swimming or boating during a storm. Electricity flows easily through water and also through you if you are in the water. Swimming, wading, snorkeling and scuba diving are not safe. If you are in a boat, get below deck or on the beach. Do not stand in puddles even if wearing rubber boots.

- During severe storms, do not use electrical appliances or the telephone. Lightning can strike outside and follow the wires into your home.

- Also, protect equipment with surge suppressors and unplug your computer and other sensitive electrical equipment to avoid damage caused by lightning surges.

- Avoid the shower, sink and bathtub. Lightning surges also can occur inside your home by traveling through your plumbing.

- Keep away from fallen power lines and treat them all as if they were energized and dangerous. If you are in an automobile that is hit by fallen wires, do not leave the vehicle. If you must leave because of a life-threatening situation, use extreme caution. Jump out and off with both feet at the same time so you are completely clear of the vehicle before you touch the ground. Never touch the vehicle and the ground at the same time.

- Sign up for a first aid/CPR class. Check with your local hospital community education department or the Red Cross for availability. Your knowledge could save a life.

- For boaters, have a weather radio on board, and don't be on the water when a storm comes up.

Lightning Myths:

- **Lightning strikes the highest point: FALSE**. Lightning strikes the best conductor of electricity, and sometimes that can be a human being.

- **Lightning never strikes in the same place twice: FALSE**. Buildings as high as the Carlton Centre in Johannesberg may get hit by lightning a couple of times a year.

- **You can buy surge protectors or suppressors to protect your appliances and home electronics: FALSE**. Experts say that surge protectors are not ideal as protection against lightning and power surges. While there are many good devices on the market, there is no guarantee of absolute protection from lightning or electrical surges.

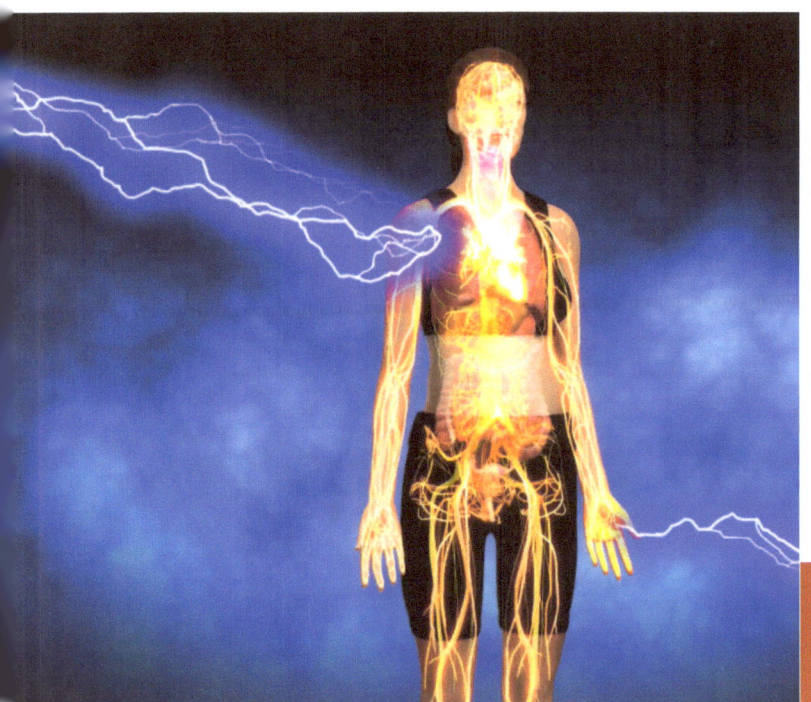

Should you have any questions about lightning and risk transfer, call 0861 SATIB 4U (0861 728 4248) or visit www.satib.com.

In Africa it is best to follow a leader.

The importance of having a specialist broker in Tourism and Leisure is undeniable. SATIB pioneered cover for this industry nearly 25 years ago and continues to stay ahead through innovation and regular consultations with clients and cover providers across Africa. Our established relationships with international and local insurers and our intimate understanding of the industry allows us to provide tailored products, ample capacity and exceptional services that ensure your business is secure. Make sure your Insurance Broker is in tune with your needs. Give us a call today and become one of our esteemed clients.

ROAD TEST
Ford Everest

The much anticipated all new Ford Everest has arrived and impressively so. The seven seater 4x4 SUV comes with a host of new features making it class-leading and a huge leap forward from the previous model launched locally in mid 2010, writes **Steve Conradie**.

The launch took place in the beautiful winelands of the Western Cape. The long and winding roads through the escarpment were ideal for road testing. The comfort and road handling proved exceptional and I quickly found myself so confident in the Everest's capability that my concentration was easily distracted by the mesmerizing scenery.

Ford have been aggressive in their approach utilizing an arson of features offered in many of their other models ensuring this vehicle will turn heads!

For now, South Africa will only receive two models, the XLT and the higher spec'd Limited, both powered by a refined, next generation 3.2-litre five-cylinder Duratorq TDCi turbodiesel engine delivering 147kW and an impressive 470Nm. Well balanced for both daily commuting, weekend 4x4ing and towing. The 6 speed automatic gearbox with Sport Shift proved a perfect match with unbelievably smooth transitions and adaptive gear selection.

There is a smaller four-cylinder 2.2-litre Duratorq TDCi turbodiesel on offer but not available in South Africa just yet.

On first impression you can quickly see that Ford have used the same successful aggressive style found in the Ranger. It handsomely displays the largest Ford badge found outside of the USA.

Both models come standard with some of the most diverse features I have seen on a mid-market SUV. The Electric Power Assist Steering (EPAS) with Drift Compensation Technology on the Limited was both impressive and scary. The Lane Keeping System which includes Lane Keeping Aid, Lane Departure Warning & Driver Alert System and Blind Spot Monitoring (BLIS) with Cross Traffic Alert was jaw dropping but too regulatory for my liking

The suspension impressed me the most. The front has Independent suspension with anti-roll, while coil springs with Watt links are fitted in the rear, making the ride firm yet extremely comfortable with almost zero rollover experienced during testing.

The large 20 inch wheels (Limited) not only add to the aggressive appeal but add real ride comfort, especially over rough terrain.

Other standard features include 7 Airbags, Electronic Stability Programme (ESP), Anti-lock Brake System (ABS), Electronic Brakeforce Distribution (EBD),Hill Launch Assist (HLA), Hill Descent Control (HDC) Roll-Over Mitigation (ROM), Emergency Brake Warning on a head up display, Trailer Sway Control (TSC), Adaptive Load Control, Remote entry with selective unlocking and flip key.

The interior is huge. Both the second and third row seats fold flat offering a spacious 2010 litres of packing space.

The steering wheel almost feels too small for an SUV but is sporty and has more buttons than an F1.

The dash and trim are classy with a great balance of soft touch and practical plastic complemented by just the right amount of chrome trim.

Ford uses it's SYNC2™ in car entertainment which includes Radio/CD/MP3; 8" touch screen; 10 speakers; x2 USB, SD card slot, aux connector, Bluetooth and voice control.

The first and second rows seats have longer than average tracking giving the driver and passengers plenty of leg room. The second row has it's own climate control. The Limited has handy power fold third row seats and power liftgate.

Functional additions include plenty of storage compartments throughout, cup holders on all three rows of seats and strategic cargo fasting points in the rear.

Additional power points are found in the second row and load compartment.

The Dual Panel Powered Moonroof, one of the few options offered on the Limited, framed in black sound absorbing trim is great for keeping the kids entertained exploring the evening sky.

Due to unexpected bad weather the 4x4 route had to be canceled. This was disappointing. As a 4x4 traditionalist my key intent on this launch was to put this high tech, "beautiful looking", family car through it's paces and see how it compared off-road to its big brother the Ranger.

The Terrain Management System (TMS), similar to that found in the Discovery, makes this technically a very capable off roader. The four settings; normal, snow/gravel/grass, sand and rock; assists the novice in approaching any obstacle with confidence pre-selecting the correct gear, throttle response, electronic traction control and engine management.

With 225mm ground clearance, 25 degree departure angle, 21 degree ramp-over angle, a 25 degree approach angle and 800mm water wading the Everest has all the necessary specs to handle most terrain. The protruding plastic side steps may prove problematic though. I would have preferred stainless steel rock sliders.

Towing is rated at a whopping 3000kg. I look forward to seeing the results of a towing test as this could be a great tow vehicle.

With the launch of the new Toyota Fortuner just around the corner it will be interesting to see if the Everest has the same impact on their rival as did the Ranger have on the Hilux.

For R593 900 for the XLT and R643 900 for the Limited you get a lot of car for your money. Maybe too much car?

*About the author: Tattler correspondent **Steve Conradie** is a seasoned 4x4 reviewer and Director at Drive South Africa www.drivesouthafrica.co.za*

www.ingramcontent.com/pod-product-compliance
Lightning Source LLC
Chambersburg PA
CBHW050423180526
45159CB00005B/2384